All About Hand-Blown Glass

Madison Spielman

Table of Contents

History of Glassblowing

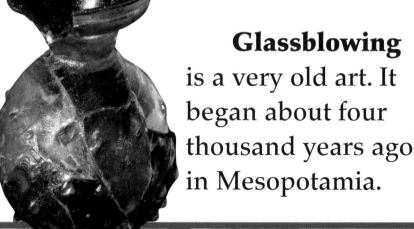

Glassblowing is a very old art. It began about four thousand years ago in Mesopotamia.

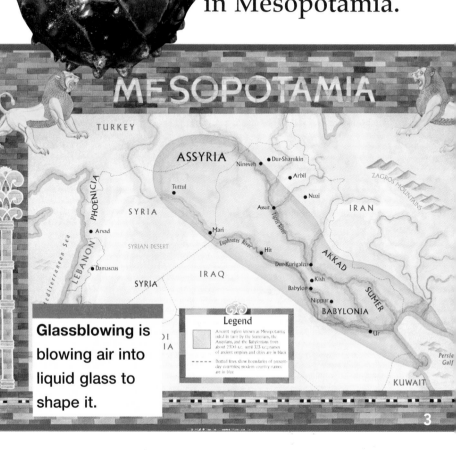

Glassblowing is blowing air into liquid glass to shape it.

The first popular use of glass was in ancient Rome. This is because the first metal pipe for blowing glass was invented in Rome. The Romans were able to make glass easily and well.

A New World of Glass

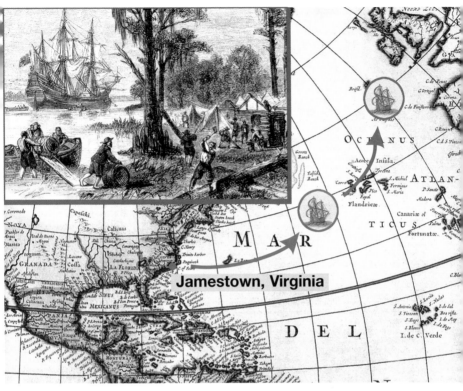

Jamestown, Virginia

Glassblowing was one of the first businesses in the New World. Captain John Smith brought **gaffers** from Europe. Gaffers are glassblowers. They built their factory near the sandy shores of Jamestown.

Long Ago

Today

Many more people in the past knew how to blow glass than people do today. But gaffers now still blow glass in much the same way they did long ago.

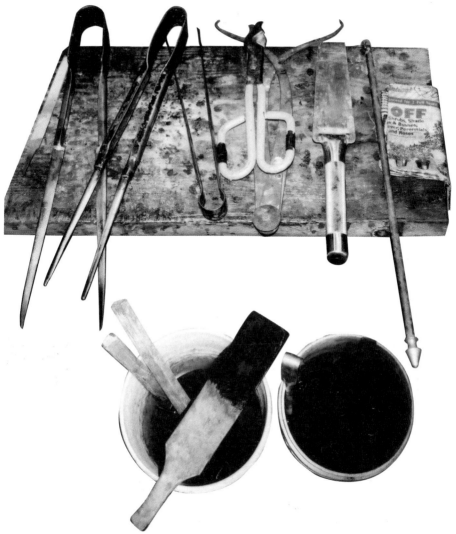

Gaffers today still use tools very much like the Romans did. Glassblowing has not changed much over time.

Glassblowing Today

The main things needed to make glass are sand, lime, soda ash, potash, and very high heat.

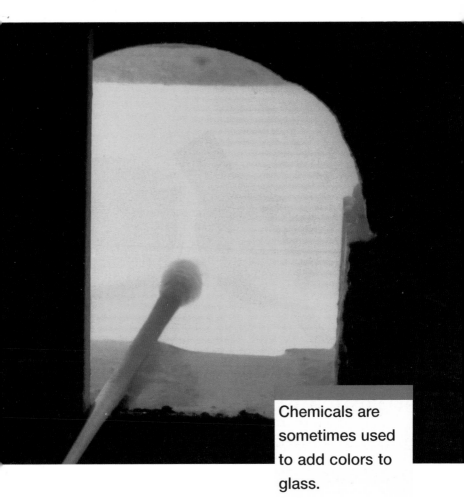

Chemicals are sometimes used to add colors to glass.

How do these ingredients
become something made of
glass? Read on to find out.

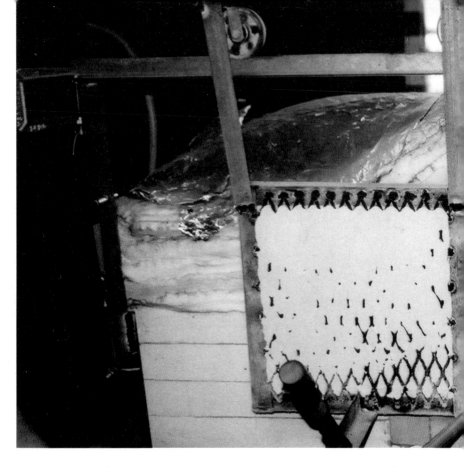

The ingredients are mixed together and heated.

Today, gas **furnaces** are used to make the heat. In the past, very hot wood fires were built in brick ovens.

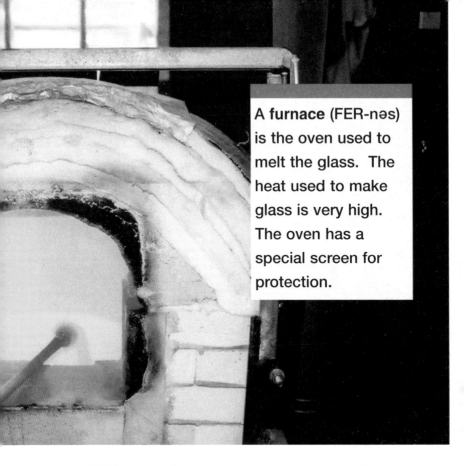

A **furnace** (FER-nəs) is the oven used to melt the glass. The heat used to make glass is very high. The oven has a special screen for protection.

When the temperature is high enough, the ingredients melt together to make liquid glass.

Gaffers must be very careful not to burn themselves!

The gaffer picks up a small amount of glass on the end of a blowpipe. This is called a **gather**.

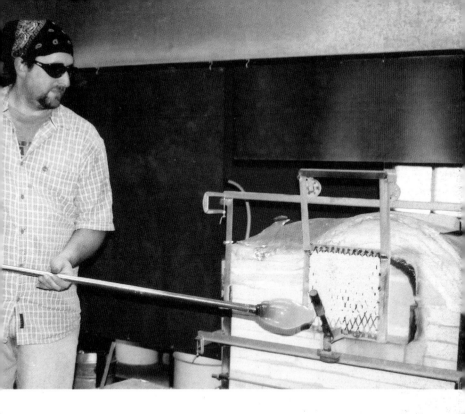

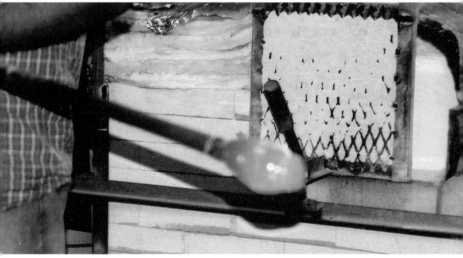

Then the gather is rolled against a smooth, flat table or paddle. This shapes the glass and cools it a bit.

Next, the gaffer blows into the blowpipe to make a bubble.

The bubble size depends on the size of the thing the gaffer wants to make.

The gaffer keeps reheating the glass, blowing into it, and shaping it.

There are plenty of tools to help do this. Molds and scissors are two of them. The gaffer can also sit in a special chair. It has long arms to help hold the blowpipe.

Soon the piece of glass
begins to take shape.

More tools are used to get it just right.

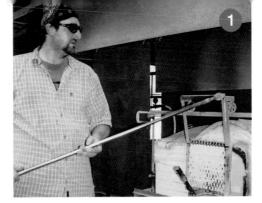

Stems, handles, and other pieces can be added to the glass with more gathers. The pictures here show the steps to add a handle.

The last step is cooling the glass. Glass cooled too quickly will shatter. So, the gaffer puts it in a special **kiln** for one or more days.

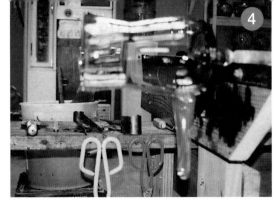

The annealing **kiln** heats and cools the glass slowly to make it sturdy.

Hand-Blown Art

In the past, blown glass was usually made into things for everyday use like bowls or dishes. Today, some hand-blown glass is still used that way. But much of it is art.

Art shops and museums are filled with beautiful pieces of hand-blown glass. They are true works of art!

Glossary

blowpipe

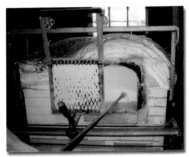

furnace

gaffers

gather

kiln